TALK TRIGGERS

by Thom and Joani Schultz

Family Tree™

Group
Loveland, Colorado

Talk Triggers

Copyright © 1989 by Thom and Joani Schultz

First Printing

Designed by Judy Atwood Bienick

Scripture quotations are from the Holy Bible, New International Version. Copyright © 1973, 1978, 1984 International Bible Society. Used by permission of Zondervan Bible Publishers.

Schultz, Thom.
    Talk Triggers / by Thom and Joani Schultz.
         p.   cm.
    ISBN 0-931529-91-3
    1. Teenagers—United States—Family relationships—
Miscellanea.
    2. Intergenerational relations—United States—Miscellanea.
    3. Communication in the family—United States—
Miscellanea.
    4. Conversation—Miscellanea.   I. Schultz, Joani Lillevold,
1953-   . II. Title.
HQ796.S4174   1989
646.7'8—dc20   89-7561
                                                              CIP

Printed in the United States of America

Contents

Introduction

Over the years we've made a discovery about parents and teenagers: Parents *want* to talk with their teenagers, and teenagers *want* to talk with their parents. But they often don't know how to get started.

Sometimes parents and teenagers just need an excuse to talk. A reason to communicate. Something to trigger a conversation.

That's the purpose of this book. *Talk Triggers* provides the spark to ignite fun, enlightening conversations. It's packed with more than 200 questions. Some silly. Some serious. All thought-provoking or faith-provoking.

A couple years ago we talked with a church youth group about parent-teenager communication. We gave the young people each a list of questions like those in this book to take home and explore with their parents. The following week, a 16-year-old girl from the group told us, "I've never talked with my mom like that before! I learned things about her that I never knew. It was great!" God used a simple tool—a few questions—to unlock a parent-teenager relationship.

Since that time we've been writing a regular column called "Talk Triggers" in Parents & Teenagers newsletter. The warm response to that column encouraged us to write this book.

We've collected all sorts of questions. Some ask about your past. Some ask you to muse about the future. Some pose wild scenarios in which to imagine yourself. And some questions ask you to clarify your faith and understanding of God. Your answers will cause you to think, to apply your values, to laugh—and to learn a lot more about your family.

Use this book to ask questions you've always been embarrassed to ask. You'll find questions about money, grades, sex, God and family memories. And you'll discover questions that'll give you an excuse to tell how much you love one another.

So, have fun with these questions. Look for surprises! And may God enrich your relationship as parents and teenagers.

Hints for Using These Questions

Before launching into the book, use these suggestions to get the most out of *Talk Triggers*:

1. Browse through the pages. We don't intend that you use this book from beginning to end. Flip through the pages and choose questions that catch your eye and interest. That way you select what you'd like to learn about your parent or teenager.

2. Watch for the ZINGERS! Every so often you'll notice boxed questions with a lot of punch. Each one designates who it's for. For example, "ZINGER to ask your TEENAGER" means the parent asks this one.

3. Trade off. Enhance fun and discovery by taking turns asking and answering questions. Pass the book around. Maybe you'll want to hear someone else's answer to a question you were just asked.

4. Don't look for a right answer.
The questions are designed to open up discussion—not to be weapons for attack. Most questions don't have right or wrong answers. If you attack someone's answer, you'll only cut off the dialogue, and no one will want to play anymore. Save the volatile debates for another time.

5. Don't allow simple "yes" or "no" answers. Use follow-ups such as: "Tell me more" or "Explain why you feel that way; I'd really like to know." Don't use sarcasm or vindictiveness. Probe for an explanation, because you genuinely want to build a closer relationship with your parent or teenager.

6. Listen. Beware of butting in with your feelings or answers when someone else is talking. Take advantage of this time to learn more about the other person. You can't do that if you're doing all the talking.

7. Enjoy each other. Whenever we hear someone answer questions like these, we're fascinated, intrigued and delighted to learn what makes someone else tick. It's fun! It's like finding an unexpected treasure. So laugh together. Cry together. Just enjoy discovering more about your God-given relationship.

☐   ☐   ☐

Use this book anytime. Keep it at the dinner table. Or in the car. Or on the television. Turn the television off once in a while for an intriguing time of questions and answers. You'll be surprised how time will fly.

Pray that God will use this book to cement your family relationships. Allow God's spirit to blow through your conversations. Then give thanks that you are the parents and teenagers God put together!

Talk Triggers: the Questions

1.

If you could become any member of our family, who would you choose? Why?

2.

If you brought three dirty, homeless people home for Thanksgiving dinner, how do you think our family would react?

3.

Ephesians 6:1-3 says: "Children, obey your parents in the Lord, for this is right. 'Honor your father and mother'—which is the first commandment with a promise—'that it may go well with you and that you may enjoy a long life on the earth.'" According to this, how long do you think you'll live? Why?

4.

Which is your favorite room in our home? Why?

5.

Which TV family is our family most like? most unlike? Why?

6.

If you could invent a cure for pimples, but you'd have to suffer from acne the rest of your life, would you do it? Why or why not?

Zinger to ask your TEENAGER

7. Imagine the teacher leaves the room during a final exam. While he is away, every student cheats. When the teacher returns, he catches *you* cheating. The teacher tells you that you just failed the test, and asks you if anyone else in the room cheated. What would you say? Now imagine that a $15,000 scholarship is to be given to the top 10 students in this classroom. But the only way you'll be eligible is if everyone is penalized for cheating. Would this change your decision to report the other students' cheating? Why or why not?

8.

Which of these bears best describes you right now?
- a teddy bear
- a polar bear
- a grizzly bear
- a koala bear

9.

If you could ask God one question, what would it be? Why?

10.

If your friend loaned you his or her favorite shirt, and you ruined it—but you could replace it without your friend finding out—what would you do? Why?

Zinger to ask your PARENT

11. Imagine the school principal calls and asks, "Why did you let your teenager outside looking like this?" What would you say?

12.

If you could always drive 15 miles per hour over the speed limit and never get caught, would you? Why or why not?

13.

What's your favorite day of the week? Why?

14.

What's the hardest thing for you to talk about in our family? Why?

15.

To prove your love to someone, would you shave your head? Why or why not?

16.

Describe where you think you'll be and what you'll be doing in 10 years.

Zinger to ask your PARENT

17. If someone offered you $20,000 to wear clothes like mine for a year, but you weren't allowed to explain why you were doing it, would you? Why or why not?

Zinger to ask your TEENAGER

18. If someone offered you $5,000 to wear clothes like mine for a year, but you weren't allowed to explain why you were doing it, would you? Why or why not?

19.

Imagine our pastor just delivered the worst sermon you ever heard. On your way out of church the pastor asks, "How'd you like my sermon?" What would you say?

20.

When was the last time you felt embarrassed? Tell about it.

21.

What's one family tradition you never want to give up? Why? What's one tradition you could live without? Why?

22.

Should people kiss on the first date? Why or why not?

23.

If you had your choice of staying as you are or becoming a very attractive member of the opposite sex, which would you choose? Why?

24.

If you could take one family photo to keep and show someone 100 years from now, what would we be doing in the photo?

Zinger to ask your TEENAGER

25. If you could take a pill that would give you a beautiful or handsome body, but it would make you unable to have children in the future, would you do it?

26.

If you could tell people when and how they were going to die, would you tell them? Would you want to know when and how you'll die? Why or why not?

27.

Why does God allow tragedies to happen?

28.

What's more important: to be able to laugh or to be able to cry? Why?

29.

If the schools made a rule that a report card could be seen by only the parent or the student, who should be allowed to see it? Why?

Zinger to ask your PARENT

30. What fad did you take part in as a teenager that now embarrasses you?

31.

What's the perfect age to be? Why?

32.

When does a person become an adult? Explain your answer.

33.

If you could set the perfect curfew time, when would it be? What would be the appropriate punishment for violating the curfew time?

34.

When was the last time you felt really hurt? Tell about it.

Zinger to ask your PARENT

35. If you could be a teenager in our family for a day, what would you do? Why?

Zinger to ask your TEENAGER

36. If you could be a parent for a day, what would you do? Why?

37.

If you didn't have to work for a living, what would you do? Why?

38.

What's your least favorite chore around the home? Why?

39.

If you could visit any place in the world, where would you go? Would you still go if you knew you could never return? Explain your answer.

Zinger to ask your PARENT

40. How would you react if I said I planned to marry someone of another race?

41.

If a co-worker asked you to cover up for him or her so the boss wouldn't get mad, would you do it? Why or why not?

42.

Would you rather live to age 35 as a millionaire, or to age 85 on meager means? Why?

43.

If school officials suspect widespread drug use, should they be allowed to search all students' lockers? Why or why not?

44. If you had to choose between straight A's or a drivers license and straight C's, which would you choose? Why?

45.

If you could spend 24 hours with anyone in the world, who would it be? What would you do together?

46.

If you could purchase a video of your friends telling exactly what they think of you, would you buy it? Why or why not?

47.

Which family vacation or "play time" do you most remember? Why?

Zinger to ask your PARENT

48. Did your parents give you "the birds and bees" talk? When? How did you feel about it? What do you remember about it?

49.

Why do you suppose God asks us to save sex for marriage?

50.

If you went to a party and realized you didn't know anyone, would you leave, or stay and get acquainted? Why?

Zinger to ask your PARENT

51. What do you think worries me most about you?

zinger to ask your TEENAGER

52. What do you think worries me as your parent most about you?

53.

If you won a $1 million sweepstakes, what would you do with the money?

54.

If you could end all wars by killing one innocent person, would you do it? Why or why not? What if that person were your closest friend? your worst enemy?

55.

Which is worse: a teenager cheating on a test or a parent making unauthorized, personal long-distance calls on the company phone? Why?

56.

What's your favorite holiday? Why?

57.

If you knew Jesus would return tomorrow, what would you do today?

Zinger to ask your **TEENAGER**

58. If you could choose my profession for me, what would you choose? Why?

Zinger to ask your PARENT

59. If you could choose my profession for me, what would you choose? Why?

60.

For $20,000 would you stay for a month in a dark cave with no contact with the outside world? Why or why not?

61.

If you could get together with one old friend, who would it be? What would you do together?

62.

If you could exchange wardrobes with anybody, whose would it be? Why?

63.

Do competition and Christianity mix? Why or why not?

64.

If you were the judge in a drunk-driving case involving a death, what punishment would you give the convicted drunk driver? Why?

Zinger to ask your PARENT

65. If you had the opportunity to be graded on your parenting performance by a national review board, would you do it? Why or why not? Would it make any difference if you were required to show your grades to me?

66.

If you could relive one day of your life, which day would it be?

67.

If a foreign exchange student lived with our family for a year, what would be the first thing he'd tell his parents back home about our family?

68.

What has been the hardest thing about being a part of our family in the past few years? What's the best thing?

69.

When was the last time you felt put down? Tell about it.

Zinger to ask your TEENAGER

70. Imagine you've been grounded for the weekend. But on Saturday night you sneak out and buy a lottery ticket that instantly wins $25,000. Would you tell me? What do you think would happen?

71.

Jesus said, "Unless you change and become like little children, you will never enter the kingdom of heaven" (Matthew 18:3). What do you think he meant? How are you like a little child?

72.

If you would declare a family holiday, what would it be? What would you call it?

73.

If you were offered $5,000 to take a two-hour bath with thousands of leeches, would you do it? Why or why not?

74.

If you won a full scholarship to the college of your choice, but you discovered someone had mixed up the files and the scholarship really belonged to someone else, what would you do? Why?

Zinger **to ask your PARENT**

75. Does being a Christian make it easier or harder for you at work? Explain.

Zinger to ask your TEENAGER

76. Does being a Christian make it easier or harder for you at school? Explain.

77.

Imagine you looked out a window and saw our neighbors walking around in their home unclothed. Would you watch them if you knew they couldn't see you? Why or why not?

78.

What family pictures embarrass you most? Why?

79.

Do you act differently around church people than you do around other people? Explain.

80.

What's the most memorable gift I ever gave you?

Zinger to ask your PARENT

81. Have you ever attended a high school reunion? If so, which of your old schoolmates surprised you most? Why?

82.

If, during the filming of a national TV show, the camera caught you picking your nose, how much money would you offer to keep that scene off the air?

83.

How would your life be different if God didn't exist?

Zinger to ask your TEENAGER

84. If you had the power to give everyone in your school A's—but they didn't deserve it—would you do it? Why or why not?

85.

Under what conditions should parents have the right to snoop in their teenager's dresser drawers?

86.

If you could receive at least 30 compliments a day, but people were paid to praise you, would you still want those compliments? Why or why not?

87.

If you could choose one of the following, which would you choose?
- a sparkling personality with an ugly body
- a beautiful body with a dull personality

Zinger to ask your **PARENT**

88. If you could have one positive quality I have as your teenager, what would it be? Why?

Zinger to ask your TEENAGER

89. If you could have one positive quality that I have as your parent, what would it be? Why?

90.

If everybody at a summertime party wanted to go skinny-dipping, would you join them? Why or why not?

91.

When has someone really hurt you with his or her teasing? Tell about it.

92.

If a cashier gave you $5 too much change, what would you do?

Zinger to ask your PARENT

93. Imagine you're trying to sell our house, and you agree over the phone to sell it to someone. But 10 minutes later someone else calls and makes an offer $20,000 higher, what would you do?

94.

If 10 people praise you and one criticizes you, which comments do you think about the most?

95.

What hardship has strengthened our family the most?

96.

When you get to heaven, what personal qualities will the angels applaud you for?

97.

If you were an animal instead of a person, what would you be? Why?

98.

If you could buy a pocket lie detector that would beep every time someone told a lie, would you buy and use it? Why or why not?

99.

What would you tell a dying aunt who wants to leave all her savings to a TV evangelist instead of to you and our family?

Zinger to ask your TEENAGER

100. Jesus befriended the outcasts of his day. If he were to visit your school, who might he befriend? How would that make you feel? Would you be willing to befriend that outcast for Jesus' sake?

101.

Which is worse: telling a "white lie" or hurting someone's feelings? Why?

102.

Picture one of our relatives who's a little strange. Imagine we have been invited over for a nice dinner. On your plate you find an eight-inch hair in your lemon Jello. What do you do?

103.

If our home were burning and you could escape with only one item, what would it be? Why would you choose that?

104.

What's worse to fail at: a sport, a friendship or a test? Why?

105.

If you had the power to exterminate any type of music, what would you eliminate? Why?

Zinger to ask your PARENT

106. If you were cleaning my room and found a piece of jewelry that had been stolen from a local jewelry store, what would you do?

107.

Is it more important for you to hang around with Christian friends or non-Christian friends? Explain.

108.

If someone offered you $20,000 to act like a drunk at your own wedding, would you do it? Why or why not?

Zinger **to ask your TEENAGER**

109. If you were cleaning our home and found my diary from my teenage years, would you read it without my permission? Why or why not?

110.

James 1:19 says, "Everyone should be quick to listen, slow to speak and slow to become angry." What makes this verse difficult to follow?

111.

If your best friend began dealing drugs, would your friendship continue? Why or why not?

112.

What's the best birthday you remember? What made it so special?

113.

If you were riding with us and a new friend in our car, and suddenly a foul odor drifted through the air, would you say anything? What?

114.

How much should teenagers know about their parents' financial situation? Why?

Zinger to ask your **PARENT**

115. Is it easier to be a teenager's mother or father? Why?

Zinger to ask your TEENAGER

116. Is it easier to be a teenage son or a teenage daughter?

117.

Would you acknowledge your faith in God if it meant you'd be arrested and imprisoned for five years? Explain.

118.

If you could be launched 2,000 years into the future or 2,000 years into the past, which would you choose? Why?

Zinger to ask your PARENT

119. Jesus said, "Love your enemies" (Matthew 5:44). How do you do that at work?

120.

If you could relive one moment of your life, what would it be? Why?

121.

If a good friend had bad breath, what would you do?

Zinger to ask your TEENAGER

122. If you agreed to go to the prom with someone, then got an invitation later from someone you liked a lot better, what would you do?

123.

If you'd been present at Jesus' Crucifixion, what would you have done?

124.

Is it currently too easy to get a divorce? Explain.

125.

If you could exchange bodies with anyone, who would you choose? Why?

126. Complete this sentence: I'm most proud of my teenager when . . .

Zinger to ask your TEENAGER

127. Complete this sentence: I'm most proud of my parent when . . .

128.

Do you think God would send a disease like AIDS to punish homosexuals and drug users? Why or why not?

129.

Should schools be allowed to distribute birth control devices to students without the parents' permission? Why or why not?

Will people who've never heard of Jesus Christ go to hell? Explain.

Zinger to ask your TEENAGER

131. If you discovered that your locker partner had stashed drugs in your locker, what would you do?

Zinger to ask your
PARENT

132. If you found out your boss was investing company profits in illegal activities, what would you do?

133.

If God were to bless you with fame or fortune, which would you choose? Why?

134.

What one thing would you change about our family right now?

135.

If your favorite pet could be a heart donor, would you sacrifice its life for an ailing, weird neighbor down the street? Why or why not?

Zinger to ask your PARENT

136. What's the most embarrassing thing I could do in front of your friends?

Zinger to ask your TEENAGER

137. What's the most embarrassing thing I could do in front of your friends?

138.

If your boss offered you a raise, but you knew you didn't deserve it, would you accept it?

139.

What's the best thing about our church?

140.

If you went to a violent movie and found out halfway through that the violence was not staged, but actual, would you stay and watch the rest of the movie? Why or why not?

Zinger to ask your TEENAGER

141. When you have your own children, how will you raise them differently than you've been raised?

142.

What difference has Jesus made in your life?

143.

If you found out that your best friend is homosexual, how would you react?

144.

1 Corinthians 13:4-7 says: "Love is patient, love is kind. It does not envy, it does not boast, it is not proud. It is not rude, it is not self-seeking, it is not easily angered, it keeps no record of wrongs. Love does not delight in evil but rejoices with the truth. It always protects, always trusts, always hopes, always perseveres." How is love in our family like a part of that passage?

Zinger **to ask your PARENT**

145. What makes it hard to tell me you love me?

Zinger to ask your TEENAGER

146. What makes it hard to tell me you love me?

147.

Is it easier for you to give or receive compliments? Why?

148.

If you knew you'd be sentenced to a week in jail if you'd return an overdue library book, would you return it or keep it? Explain.

149.

When was the last time you felt really forgiven? Tell about it.

Zinger to ask your TEENAGER

150. If you could prevent one of the following, which would you choose? Why?

● a famine in Africa that would kill 40,000 people

● food poisoning in your school cafeteria that would kill all the students except you

151.

If your friends knew everything about you, would they still be your friends? Explain.

152.

Do you like your name? What would you change it to if you could?

Zinger to ask your PARENT

153. How are you a different parent from your own parents?

154.

If you had a vivid dream—three nights in a row—in which God asked you to leave our family, give up all your possessions, and become a missionary in a tiny village in New Guinea, would you do it? Why or why not?

155.

Aside from family members, who would you turn to for advice about a big problem?

Zinger to ask your TEENAGER

156. If you fell in love with a non-Christian, would you marry him or her?

157.

If you could be a scuba diver or a sky diver, which would you be? Why?

158.

Who's someone you now like, but didn't like when you first met him or her? Why?

159.

Have you felt closer to God through your successes or through your failures? Explain.

160.

Who's worse to be around: a slob or a perfectionist? Why?

Zinger to ask your PARENT

161. What's one thing you did in high school that you've always regretted?

162.

If a reporter on national television asked you to describe the best thing about our family, what would you say?

163.

If you were starving on a desert island, would you eat your dead friend in order to survive? Why or why not?

164.

Who's someone who doesn't know how much he or she means to you? Why?

Zinger to ask your PARENT

165. If you knew I would die in a year, would you do anything differently?

Zinger to ask your **TEENAGER**

166. If you knew I would die in a year, would you do anything differently?

167.

If you were jolted with a severe electric shock every time you made reference to your faith, God, Jesus or the Holy Spirit, would you continue to witness? Why or why not?

168.

If you owned a rare coin worth $10,000, would you sell it now or wait 10 years when it may be worth twice as much? Why?

169.

If you could double your beauty, but it would cost you half your intelligence, would you do it? Why or why not?

Zinger to ask your TEENAGER

170. Imagine you're on your first date with someone you really like. As you sit down in a restaurant the vinyl seat makes an embarrassing sound. What would you do or say?

Zinger to ask your PARENT

171. Ephesians 6:4 says: "Fathers, do not exasperate your children." What does that mean to you?

172.

Would you rather have one really close friend or dozens of friends with whom you're not very close? Why?

173.

If someone offered you $2,000 to wear the same clothes every day for a month without washing them, and you couldn't tell anyone why you were doing it, would you do it? Why or why not?

174.

Imagine you're competing in the Olympics. You realize the only way you can win is by taking steroids. Would you take them if you were certain that no one would ever know? Why or why not?

Zinger to ask your TEENAGER

175. If you had the choice of getting an A average but then forgetting most of what you learned, or a C average and remembering most of what you learned, which would you choose? Why?

176.

Which of the following would bring you more satisfaction? Why?
- Buying a dream car
- Spending a week fixing up a poor family's home

177.

How does a person get to heaven?

Zinger to ask your **PARENT**

178. Complete this sentence: Three wishes or hopes I have for my teenager's future are . . .

179.

Have you ever popped a grape or strawberry into your mouth in a supermarket without paying for it? Do you consider that stealing? Would Jesus be caught doing that? Why or why not?

180.

What's your biggest worry? Why?

181.

Imagine you're in a packed movie theater. What would you do if the stranger next to you talked throughout the movie?

182.

If you could be famous, what would you like to be famous for? Why?

183.

What do you think a messy bedroom says about the person who lives in it?

Zinger to ask your **TEENAGER**

184. What's one thing you need right now from me?

Zinger to ask your PARENT

185. What's one thing you need right now from me?

186.

If you could abolish one family rule, what would it be? Why?

187.

Jesus said: "Anyone who loves his father or mother more than me is not worthy of me; anyone who loves his son or daughter more than me is not worthy of me" (Matthew 10:37). How do you react to this passage? How does a person know that nothing surpasses his or her love for Christ?

188.

When you die, do you want your bodily organs donated for scientific research? Why or why not?

Zinger to ask your PARENT

189. What has surprised you most about being a parent?

190.

What do you think of parents who believe they're guarding their teenagers from drugs by sponsoring supervised beer parties at their homes?

191.

If you had a senile grandparent who behaved unusually, would you want him or her to live with our family? Why or why not?

192.

If you could read someone's mind, whose would you choose? Why?

193.

If you knew that eating health foods—and cutting out such things as hamburgers—would add 10 years to your life, would you do it? Why or why not?

194.

Imagine a group kidnaps a family member and demands that you drop off a large sum of money at a certain spot. The kidnappers tell you that if you call the police they'll kill the captive. Would you call the police? Why or why not?

Zinger to ask your **TEENAGER**

195. If someone arranged a blind date for you, would you go? Why or why not?

196.

Which of the following is closest to the truth about why some people are poor? Explain your answer.

- They're lazy.
- They don't know any better.
- They don't have opportunities to improve their lives.
- They've been treated unfairly by society.

197.

Can single people be as happy and fulfilled in life as married people? Explain your answer.

198.

When was the last time you felt falsely accused of something? How did you respond?

199.

If you could receive $10,000 for appearing in a TV documentary, would you do it—knowing that a hidden camera and microphone would record your every move and word for the next month? Why or why not?

200.

If a man visited our home claiming to be Christ, how would you verify he was telling the truth?

201.

If you witnessed a gang murder, would you tell the police who did it, knowing that the gang might seek revenge against you? Why or why not?

Zinger to ask your TEENAGER

202. Do you think you'll live in this area the rest of your life? If so, why? If not, where do you see yourself living? Why?

Zinger to ask your
PARENT

203. How is marriage different from what you expected it to be?

204.

Is suicide more an act of courage or cowardice? Why?

205.

When eating at a restaurant with a friend, do you usually pray before you eat? Why or why not?

206.

What's worse: to be very fat or to suffer from an eating disorder that makes you very skinny? Why?

207.

What brings true happiness in life?

Zinger to ask your TEENAGER

208. If you were married and you became attracted to someone other than your spouse, what would you do?

209.

Would you want to know the sex of your unborn child? Why or why not?

210.

If you had to choose between dropping out of school to help our family pay bills or staying in school and living in poverty, which would you choose? Why?

Zinger to ask your TEENAGER

211. Would you marry someone you loved if you knew the two of you could never have children?

Zinger to ask your PARENT

212. What's one of the best memories you have of me as a baby?